How to Treat a Lady

Dating Advice for
Young Men from Older Women

Dee Ray

HOW TO TREAT A LADY
Dating Advice for Young Men from Older Women
Copyright © 2023 by Dee Ray

All rights reserved. No part of this publication may be reproduced, distributed, or transmitted in any form or by any means, including photocopying, recording, or other electronic or mechanical methods, without the prior written permission of the publisher or author, except in the case of brief quotations embodied in critical reviews and certain other noncommercial uses permitted by copyright law.

Although every precaution has been taken to verify the accuracy of the information contained herein, the author and publisher assume no responsibility for any errors or omissions. No liability is assumed for damages that may result from the use of information contained within.

ISBN-13: Paperback: 978-1-64749-873-3
          Hardback: 978-1-64749-874-0
          ePub: 978-1-64749-875-7

Printed in the United States of America

GoToPublish LLC
1-888-337-1724
www.gotopublish.com
info@gotopublish.com

Table of Contents

Introduction v
Traits the Women I've Known Want in a Man 1
How Would Your Lady Like To Be Treated? 3
How to Treat a Woman 13
On Being a Gentleman 25
How to Make an Uninterested Woman
Become Interested (By A Woman) 31
How to Treat Your Wife 33

INTRODUCTION

I suppose there have always been romantic liaisons between young men and older women since the beginning of time. But even as recently as 1967, when the movie *The Graduate* became popular, the idea was somewhat unusual and even shocking. Today, so-called "cougars" (women who hunt younger men), are discussed and photographed openly. They even have their own dedicated websites.

This book is not advocating young men get together with older women or older women hunt younger men. Rather, it contains wisdom from a number of older women (defined, by us, as 40 or better) who dated for decades, a few into the 70s. As Dee Ray points out in the first chapter, the basics have not changed much since we were young.

Our teenage and college-age children and grandchildren now date. Some things have changed: for example, going out in groups instead of pairs, equality of door-opening and payments, and girls comfortable making the first move are things that were unusual years ago, but common now. On the other hand, we see and hear young women looking for the exactly same enduring qualities in men as we do (and did), things like:

— Respect.
— Kindness.
— Consideration.
— Mutual Interests.
— A Positive Attitude.
— A Sense of Humor.

We are all concerned about the rise in violence toward girls in teenage dating relationships in recent years, and we are also concerned about books and websites which advise young men how to "get" women. While we sympathize with all the young men who do not feel comfortable approaching women and are afraid of (or stung by) being rejected, there must be a better solution in today's world than teaching catch phrases and superficial come-ons.

There are two sides to every story, and this one is written from the woman's view. Young men may be surprised at some of the specific things these women (and other women) complain about. Maybe we should recruit some psychologists and marriage counselors who have "heard it all" like we have to write another book of mutual ice-breakers, or something. Or maybe we should get some older men who have been though different ages and stages of dating to give us articles for another book, *How Would Your Man Like to Be Treated?*

We hope young men will get some new and useful ideas that will help them land the lady of their dreams in a wonderful and lasting relationship. We hope young ladies will buy a copy for their dates!

Traits the Women I've Known Want in a Man

Robbie Motter

Women want a man to be confident, be the real you.
Women want men who go the extra mile and make them feel special.
Women want their men to take time to listen to them, not always give advice.
Women want men with a sense of humor.
Women want men who are loyal – men of character.
Women want to be treated like a woman, not like a man.
Women love men with a plan, and women love men with ambition.
Women want generous men – give the woman in your life gifts.
Women want men to be true friends.
Women want to be loved despite their flaws – they need to be satisfied mentally, emotionally, and spiritually as much as physically.
Women appreciate men who are creative.
Women want men who offer a sense of security; they want to know that a partner will be there if they become sick, grow old or even flabby.

Robbie Motter has known thousands of women in her longtime role as Regional Director for the National Association for Female Executives (NAFE) and founder of numerous California women's business and professional organizations. Robbie also has a weekly radio show on which she interviews interesting women, and has won numerous local, state and national awards for her contributions to women's programs and mentoring women. For more, see www.RobbieMotter.com.

How Would Your Lady Like To Be Treated?

(15 Tips for Men Who Don't Have a Clue)
Dee Ray

It seems to me that not much has improved on the dating scene since 1980 when my husband died. He used to say:

— "I feel sorry for women; men just don't seem to get it."
— "They don't really know how to treat a lady."
— "They really should have a school for men."

Since we still don't have an etiquette school for you young fellows, I'll do my best to be helpful. I'll share the intimate details of some of my own best and worst experiences over the years, and my tips for how YOU should treat YOUR lady.

So how does a lady really want to be treated?

Tip #1: Be truly interested in her.

First off, treat her like you're interested in her as a person - not just her looks, sex, or her money. Forget about yourself for now.

Be interested in what she has to say. Treat her like she has a brain. Find out what she likes and is interested in (and don't do a phony pretend you're interested. Don't make it seem like an interview for online dating, either).

Tip #2: Don't be demeaning.

I once had a guy say to me we should date because I lived near him and, therefore, it would be more convenient for him. Now there's a real turn on! What a stupid thing to say. Made me wonder where he grew up and what kinds of manners were taught in his home. So after all these years and some recent experiences, I decided I would write an article about my experiences. Some, I think, are rather shocking.

Tip #3: Talk about things that interest your date.

Recently a longtime friend asked me to be his escort to numerous functions as his lady friend had gone to Arizona for the winter. On the way to one event, he started talking about how bulls service the cows. Really, what a perfectly dumb conversation! He seemed possessed with the subject. I finally let him know it was a ridiculous conversation.

Boy, was I happy he wasn't a boyfriend of mine! I was wondering to myself if he talked to his lady friend like this and, if so, would she be ditching him soon, or was she desperate for anything that wore pants? I know a few women like that and truly cannot understand them. Sure seems to me like a terrible trade off. It is easier to deal with things like this if your date is just a friend. Then she can feel free to tell them how utterly stupid they're acting. Bear in mind, my friends are older men, so they should know better.

    Be polite. Be yourself - don't try to impress. Talk about interesting and fun things (not ex-wives, ex-girlfriends, your problems, your past sex life. These are all turn offs - terrible turn offs. They make you look stupid and very inconsiderate). As Aristotle Onassis once said, "Don't talk about one beautiful lady when you are with another one." Nothing is more of a turnoff than talking about past relationships!

    On one occasion, a guy was proceeding to tell me about his sex life with his ex-wife. Idiot! I very sarcastically asked if he wanted to hear about my ex-husband. He stopped the conservation for the evening. When he started the same conversation at another event, I reminded him he had already told me that very inappropriate story. Then he started in telling me in great detail of a recent girlfriend. I was wondering, "Does this guy really have a brain?"

Tip #4: Don't try to show off if you don't know what you're doing.

A friend of mine needed an escort to a dance. I like to dance so I said OK. I have been taking ballroom dancing for ten years, but he immediately started telling me I was doing it wrong. He would toss me around like a sack full of potatoes and practically tear my arm out of its socket. I told him doing the tango was not throwing his butt out in a circle. I mentioned that when doing the swing, putting his arm straight out did not set me up to make a turn. He didn't like the feedback, as he thought he actually knew how to dance.

    He liked to exchange dances with other couples, thank goodness. Then he would give me a quiz on how they danced. He would tell me what was wrong with their dance and tell me the other ladies didn't like dancing with them as they had no rhythm. Really - from the expert himself.

I made a remark that one gentleman really did the foxtrot correctly. His response was it was because the guy had long legs- I reminded him that I have short legs so that really did not have anything to do with it.

When he would get off on his sexist remarks, I asked if that was all he had on his brain. One time he called me at work and said he was not feeling up to par and that he must have his period. I said "What!", and hung up. This kind of behavior is unbelievable in a guy who should know better. He told me younger women found him attractive. I said, "In your fondest dreams!"

Tip #5: Don't come on to your date too soon.

Don't be aggressive in affections when you first meet; real ladies take sex seriously, not "wham, bam, thank you ma'am." (There are exceptions, though, I know!)

I had been friends with an Italian man for years. He had a lovely wife but she died of cancer, so I took him to a dance and introduced him to a friend of mine. He really thought he was a Don Juan. He asked her for a date and they went out to dinner. They no more got in the car than he was all over her. Needless to say, that was a complete turnoff. Not such a subtle move. But, the good thing about men who behave like this, they are easy to reject – and reject she did.

This same guy was in California and a friend of mine agreed to meet him for dinner. When she took him back to his motel, he hopped on the bed and expected her to do the same. His remark was she may as well leave then and, of course, she was delighted to do so. We had a good laugh at that one.

Tip #6: If you're over thirty, be careful about hitting on younger women.

One gal sent me a cartoon saying life is too short to dance with dirty old men. I laughed when I received it, as it has proven true.

One guy started hitting on my secretary who was 25 years younger than he. Really - what an ego! If men like this only realized what a fool they make of themselves! They just don't seem to get it. Come on guys, do you really think she likes you for you? She may really want a younger stud!

One of my friends tried to tell her boss that his girlfriend was way too young for him, and he should reconsider marrying her. His response was, "Everyone is just jealous because she's younger." But three kids later, a divorce, and her leaving him for a younger guy left him bitter.

When I was young and some older guy would hit on me, it was so disgusting. My girlfriends felt the same way. If they grabbed us and kissed us, we'd immediately go to the bathroom to gag and wash our mouths off.

Tip #7: Be honest and sincere. Look for ladies who are, too.

From my experience, the men ladies should watch out for are the really smooth ones: not sincere, but great manners and very charming. To have a sincere relationship with this kind of guy, she has to be smarter than you and catch you in your own trap. Some of you are pretty deep once they get to know you, but it is hard work.

Some of you guys are so good looking the ladies never compliment you. One time I told a guy that he really was handsome. He was thrilled with the compliment and we became very good friends. My girlfriends were always trying to get him but to no avail. I was too old for him, so I introduced him to one of my very cute and very smart girlfriend. They're now married. Not that I am good at match making, but this was a no brainer.

Tip #8: Nothing is worse than a bore.

Nothing is worse than a good looking man who's a total bore. I married a guy like that when I was 19. Always a lesson in there somewhere. Mine was I had to grow up fast and be responsible. Nine years later we were divorced.

When you are dancing with a lady – dance with just her. Don't be looking around the room for someone you think will be more fascinating or better looking. Don't brag about yourself or talk about past relationships. We really don't give a dam. Like Aristotle Onassis said, "Don't talk about another beautiful woman when you are with a beautiful woman." Makes perfect sense to me!

Tip #9: Be on time.

Be on time - not early or late. I had a 6:00 PM date once with someone at who came at 3:00 - not good! I observed he was too early and his reply was, "I don't mind." What kind of comment is that? Most women want to be ready when you arrive, especially for a first date, so don't be early. And of course, don't be late. It's rude, and suggests you aren't excited to see her.

Tip #10: Dress for success.

Dress appropriately. Don't wear shorts to a dance (especially if you have bony legs!) Some men think they're acting coy, but really I feel sorry for them. If they only realized how ridiculous they look.

The rule when I grew up was when going into a building always remove your hat, but one guy I was with wore a hat into a dining room and acted upset and insulted when he was told to take it off. Baseball hats and tennis shoes might work at a sports game or McDonalds, but they're not appropriate for fine dining or the theater. What guys think is cool about pants down around their butts and baseball hat is beyond most women. Guys without pressed or clean clothes are often a turn-off, too.

Tip #11: Focus on your date; don't be looking around while you're with her.

For instance at a dance - dance with them. I have danced with some guys whose head you would swear was on a spindle. They appear to always be looking to see if there is something better. I recall one time a gentlemen telling me, "When you're with John, you're with him; but when you're with George, you're with the whole bar." Some ladies may prefer George, but most prefer John.

Tip #12: Treat women with respect.

Being with the whole bar does not appeal to me - it does to one of my gal friends. She likes being with the whole bar. At one time she had just gone through a divorce from a high powered executive and was feeling her oats. I guess everyone deals with things in their own way. I recall being on a cruise with her one time and the head of entertainment said to her, "Don't eat too much, I don't sleep well on a full stomach." Obviously she could brush if off. One time she did get heartbroken on a vacation – she took a guy seriously.

Tip #13: Be careful about "love at first sight."

Love at first sight can work: I knew within two weeks I wanted to marry my second husband. My first husband I knew at least three years - but I was too young and it was a bad match. I was 19 and he was 24. I had to be the responsible one in many ways and I did not like that. (I guess some women, I am told, like to be in total charge. I am not one of them.)

Tip #14: If you're just horny, try the gym.

I got some good advice from a man friend after my husband died. It was, "Go to the gym." He said when he first got a divorce he went through a series of dates and sex and could not even recall half of their names or even their faces. He said, he realized what a waste of time and energy that was.

Tip #15: Act like the kind of husband and father you'd like to be.

I had a very loving and respectful father which I think helps. We had five girls in our family and it was unconditional love. We all felt equal: a real talent in a father. My mom was (before her time) a real women's libber, but a sensible one. She believed in women's rights but, also, was not afraid to be "all women." Above all, men, show some manners and respect.

I don't dislike men, but some of their manners are shocking to me.

Of course being human, as we are, there are exceptions to every rule. I have had guys confess to me that their wives are not cuddly or affectionate, and I am not talking about sex. I always think these ladies don't know how lucky they are to have a guy like that. I can't imagine that, myself, unless they don't really love the man.

A happy ending (and a good model for you guys!)

I was lucky when at twenty-eight I met the man of my dreams. We had been married for fifteen years when he died. Every day was like a honeymoon - what a gift! My mother told me she had never seen me so content.

My husband was very thoughtful and fun. If I didn't like something, I only had to tell him once. He was very observant about things I liked and didn't like. We both appreciated each other and loved doing things for each other. He was very smart, and I think the sexiest thing about a man is his brain.

He never used bad language in front of any women. He treated all my lady friends with great respect, and loved talking with them. They always said to me, "You will never meet anyone like that again!" (I say there's always hope, even at my age. God works in strange and wondrous ways!)

Also, my husband was a fantastic dancer. He was a great gourmet cook. He was very appreciative of any little thing I did for him. He was a happy, fun, and very romantic guy. Gals usually like thoughtful, romantic guys; also guys who really know how to dance, and like to dance with them.

It was Dee Ray who inspired and edited this book, thinking young men may not be taught how to treat women and need some tips from women who have "been there, done that." DeeDee is a senior vice president at a prominent brokerage and investment banking firm. After being a dating widow for several years, she realized "older men" are often less savvy than the young men, although she thinks they should know better!

How to Treat a Woman

Edited by Kedrian James, Ben Rubenstein,
Flickety, Sondra C and 75 others

Treating a woman well requires a combination of common courtesy and uncommon acts of love and kindness. Follow the steps below, and soon your woman will see you for what you are: one of the good guys.

Be a Good Communicator

Communicate your feelings. Some men underestimate the importance of telling a woman how they feel. In many cases, men prefer to use actions rather than words to communicate their feelings. If that sounds like you, you should know that women need to hear "I love you" from time to time, so make it a point to express that sentiment. If you have trouble saying the words, try writing a note or getting a card to let her know how you feel.

— **The good news:** Turns out those men are more often the ones to declare feelings of love first in a relationship. Research has determined that men take only 88 days to tell their partner they love them (compared to a woman's

134) while another study says men say "I love you" first 70% of the time.

— **Watch your timing:** Women prefer to hear "I love you" after sex rather than before. It could be they distrust the words a bit if they're uttered before sex as it makes them wonder if you're saying "I love you" simply to get some action.

Be a Good Listener

Be a good listener. Everyone – not only women wants to be heard. If you know how to listen, your woman will greatly appreciate it, and the bond between you two will grow. Try these tips to be a better listener.

— **Get rid of distractions:** That might mean turning off the ballgame or ignoring the text you just got. Try to keep from interrupting unless the question is crucial to your understanding of the situation. Putting your focus completely on your woman shows her that she's important and that you value and are interested in what she has to say.

— **Read non-verbal cues:** Gestures, facial expressions and eye-movements can all be important. Don't just listen with your ears but also with your eyes so you can gain greater insight into what she's feeling.

See Things from Her Point of View

See things from her point of view. Your girlfriend or wife may be upset about something that would never trouble you, or she might describe a scenario you can't imagine being a part of – but you have to try. Put yourself in her shoes to try to understand what she's feeling.

— **Communicating more clearly:** Even if you don't agree with her reaction or her opinion, keep an open mind and let her know that in any dispute you're always on her side.

— **Refrain from solving the problem:** When a woman is talking through a problem she's facing, a man's first response is to jump in and try to solve it. That impulse comes from a good place, but it's not what a woman wants. She simply wants to be heard, so refrain from coming to the rescue with a solution for the situation. If she does ask your opinion about what she should do, feel free to offer your suggestions, but don't be offended if she chooses a different course of action.

Ask Her How She's Feeling

Ask her how she's feeling. In many cases, you'll know exactly how the woman in your life is feeling, but sometimes, especially when a relationship is new, you'll have to ask. Researchers in a study published in the journal *PLOS* showed men images of eyes belonging to men and women and discovered that it was twice as difficult for the men to accurately guess what women were feeling as it was for them to guess what the men were feeling. They also took longer attempting to interpret the women's eyes.

Fight Fair

Fight fair. Even the closest of couples will have arguments; what's important is how you talk to your woman during those disagreements. Do not call names or make threats or use physical intimidation. When the fight is over, don't hold on to hurt feelings; reach out and meet your woman halfway in making up.

Show Respect

Behave like a gentleman. Open door for your woman, hold out your hand to help her out of the car, take her coat and so on. Some of these behaviors might be labeled "old fashioned" or even be frowned on in the workplace, but if your woman feels comfortable with it, engage in some extra courtesies to make things a little easier and more comfortable for her.

Be Polite

Be polite. Women like to hear "please" and "thank you." Even if you've been dating a while or married a long time, don't throw manners out the window. Show her the same thoughtfulness you'd show anyone else.

— **Avoid using profanity:** Never use profanity or offensive slang to refer to your woman, even if you're just kidding. If you hold her in high regard, be sure your language reflects that.

Don't Change or Break Plans

Don't change or break plans. If it's an emergency or the change is completely unavoidable, of course you can break a date, but be sure to give as much advance notice as possible and offer a very good explanation and an apology.

Be On Time

Be on time. If you're running late, call as soon as you can to let her know. Everyone's time is valuable, and being somewhere when you say you will is just common courtesy. Resist the impulse to put off calling because you fear your woman will be angry. She might be, but chances are she'll be even angrier if you're not in touch.

Treat Her Family Well

Treat her family well. Even if she says that she's not close with her family, always be respectful toward them and avoid criticizing them. Family bonds can be strong, and parents and siblings can influence a woman's decision to date or dump a guy.

— If a woman has children, be friendly toward them and do your best to get to know them. Women are quick to say good-bye to men who do not treat their children with kindness. Don't ever overstep your bounds and try to parent or discipline her kids; leave that to the woman in your life.

Avoid Jealousy

Avoid jealousy. Being jealous of male friends, co-workers and exes without good reason tells a woman that you consider her to be deceitful and of low moral character. Not a message you want to send to someone you care for.

Help Around the House

Help around the house. If you two live together, pitch in on chores. Both of you are responsible for the housework. Don't expect her to constantly pick up after you. One of the surest ways to a woman's heart is with a vacuum cleaner in one hand and a box of laundry detergent in the other.

Make Her Feel Special

Acknowledge special occasions. Be sure you're ready with a card and a gift when her birthday rolls around, or it's time to celebrate Christmas or Valentine's Day. Marking these and other occasions with tokens of love and appreciation are a great way to make a woman feel special. Remember, too, that right or wrong, her family and friends will likely ask her what you got her or how the two of you celebrated. Don't put your woman on the spot by forcing her to lie or to admit that you let the occasion pass without recognition.

Celebrate Your Anniversaries

Celebrate your anniversary. Anniversaries are like mini-time machines. They allow the two of you to relive an important event (your wedding day, your first date, etc.) They're a chance to re-experience the special emotion created in and by that moment. Show the woman in your life that you value that event and all that's happened since, by doing something special on your anniversary. If you can afford it and your wife or girlfriend would enjoy it, go ahead and do something extravagant. But what can be most meaningful is a card or a conversation in which you reminisce about the good times and the growth of your relationship and your happiness.

Give Thoughtful Gifts

Give thoughtful gifts. Gifts that come from the heart are among the most appreciated. Put some time and thought into choosing something your woman would love or make something for her yourself. When you invest that kind of time and thought into gift giving, she can't help but be touched.

Give Flowers

Give flowers. Not every woman is a sucker for flowers, but the majorities really do appreciate a bouquet, especially if it's being given for no particular reason. Bring flowers on your next date or have them delivered to her home or workplace if that's appropriate. A card that says simply "Thinking of you" is enough to bring a smile to her face.

Mention Her to Your Friends

Mention her to your friends. If she's important to you, your friends should know it. That doesn't mean that you have to go on and on about her (and never discuss what happens in the bedroom with your friends), but making it clear that she's an important part of your life will make her feel special versus make

her feel like someone you want to hide or keep from your friends.

Bringing the Romance: Understand That Little Things Can Mean a Lot

Understand that little things mean a lot. While big romantic gestures may have their place, it's the little things that show a woman how much she means to you. Thoughtful acts like bringing her a cup of coffee in the morning or putting air in her car tires are very concrete ways of saying "I love you" without you having to utter a word. Be consistent. Show her in some way each day that you're thinking of her and trying to make her life a bit easier and happier.

Send a Message

Send a message. Scratch out a quick note, send her a text or fire off an email to let her know you're thinking of her. If she has a big day coming up – a job interview, a presentation at work – send her a message of encouragement and support.

Give Comptliments

Give compliments. You may never have to answer the question, "Do these pants make my butt look big?" if you're quick to compliment your woman on her appearance. Dispel any insecurities by saying nice things about parts of her body she might feel less than great about, and don't forget to compliment the things you find most attractive about her. Don't underestimate the impact of a simple "You look beautiful" – that pretty much says it all.

— If you do get the "Do these pants make my butt look big?" question, the correct answer is always "No."

— We all like to be recognized for the things that make us special, so compliment your woman for being who she is. Is she creative, fascinating, funny? Do you admire her achievements and her outlook on life? Tell her! And be sure to look her straight in the eye when you do so.

Follow Her Lead

Follow her lead. Initially, let the woman set the pace for your physical relationship. No woman wants to feel pressured to have sex before she's ready, and everyone has a different timetable for being ready. Let her know how you feel, but back off (without pouting) if she wants to wait before getting intimate.

Embrace Foreplay

Embrace foreplay. Physiologically, experts agree that foreplay is an important part of sexual health. In fact, an Australian study found that the majority of women are more aroused by the idea of foreplay than sex itself. Hold, touch and caress your partner, play games or talk dirty. If you're not sure what your woman likes, ask. Just do it outside the bedroom. It's easier to have that conversation if you're not just about to have sex.

Pop the Question

Pop the question. If you love her, you're ready to settle down and you know she's the one, and then make the commitment. If you plan to propose marriage, be sure you mean it. Buy a ring if you can, get on one knee and tell her that you can't imagine your life without her and ask if she'll do you the honor of becoming your wife.

This article is reprinted with permission from www.WikiHow.com *under the terms of its Creative Commons license. To see the original article, go to* www.wikihow.com/Treat-a-Woman.

On Being a Gentleman

Antonia Hall

Ready to win the woman of your dreams? Then you need to learn the art of treating your love interest like a lady. I commend you for such, for there really is an art to the dance between partners, and this is seldom taught to young men anymore (at least not in the western world, where few in your generation are raised with male mentors to set the record straight and help guide the way).

Additionally, there's a discrepancy in societal messages about how a man should treat a woman. Everything from toothpaste to cars is sold with sex, and the message seems to be that a real man is one who conquers. Believing such fallacies will not get you a true lady or a happy relationship. I'm going to let you in on some secrets about what a woman really wants. Basically, it comes down to men being chivalrous in all areas of his exchanges with his lady.

When my girlfriends and I sit around and talk about the way our men treat us, there are certain courtesies we're all seeking. So, let's begin with the basics of chivalry, which are not dead and do make most women feel treasured.

A real man is a gentleman. While some may consider it old fashioned, all of the women I know appreciate courtesy. Remember that you're being chivalrous out of your respect for her and because you want to treat her well, not because she is the weaker or lesser sex (as was the view in years past). I've always appreciated when the man I'm dating takes my hand, opens doors for me, pulls out chairs, and assists me with taking off and putting on my coat.

Only one gentleman I've dated has ever walked on the outside of the street, but I found the old tradition very considerate. He's confessed to me that most of the women he does this for appreciate it, no matter how strong and independent they are.

There are some other sweet things you can do to be a chivalrous gentleman and make your woman happy. Bring her flowers. Trust me, we know we can buy our own, and yet I've heard all too often how much my female friends love this simple gesture. Women appreciate unexpected gifts, at unexpected times. It lets them know you are thinking of them, even though they are not there with you.

When you take her out; be polite and say "please" and "thank you" and tell her that she looks beautiful. Let me repeat this. Tell her that she looks beautiful. These simple words work wonders. Just don't use them when she looks a mess and you both know it. Honest compliments are the key with women.

She's not the only one who needs to look good and feel good about them. Having a healthy dose of self-esteem will assist you greatly in being a gentleman and being a good partner in relationships. Take care of yourself physically, mentally, and emotionally. I'll be suggesting that you make special time for you and your lady, but it's important to take quality time to yourself as well.

As you court your potential sweetheart, remember to be easy going. She may be a hottie and makes you nervous, but that's fine! Some nervousness is a good thing, and part of the fun. Remember to breathe, and don't let things upset you easily, as this will scare her away. Make her laugh and set her at ease. Be confident, but not arrogant. Never belittle others to build yourself up. She'll see through this and recognize it as lack of self-esteem. In the end, you need to know that you deserve the girl or you'll end up sabotaging the situation with her.

The greatest chivalrous act is in your own intent, gentlemen. We lady-folk tend to be pretty intuitive, so make certain you're approaching her with the right intentions or things will go awry. Your intentions are the building blocks to the exchange with your lady.

It is imperative that you tell the truth and honor your word, or she'll feel disrespected and you'll find yourself with an upset lady. Keep your promises, and be respectful of her time and the plans you've made with her. Don't be late. If tardiness is unavoidable, then let her know and be apologetic. Send a text that you'll be late if it's only ten to fifteen minutes, and call if it's longer than that. While it may sound cliché, setting aside uninterrupted quality time just for the two of you, and arranging romantic evenings together, will be appreciated by your lady.

Another thing you can do to be a chivalrous gentleman is to listen to your woman. Everyone wants to be heard, and "he doesn't even listen to me" is one of the biggest complaints I hear from my female friends. Set aside any distractions, and avoid looking at the text that came through as she was talking.

Take an interest in her and her life. Maintain eye contact, and show that you're listening, but don't interrupt her. Respect her opinion, even if you don't agree with it. You don't need to agree on everything, and having a different point of view makes life more interesting. Don't criticize, and resist the temptation to solve all of her problems. By listening you are making space for her to be truly heard, which is often enough.

Want to show you care and really score points? One of the ways we women are made to feel that you care is by your willingness to do little things to make our lives easier. Of course you don't want to jeopardize your own well-being or be a needy doormat. It's the little things that make a big difference to women. Cook dinner for her, carry in the groceries or carry her books, thoughtfully draw her a bubble bath when she's had a long day.

What can you do to make her life easier? We are very appreciative when our guy fixes things around the house, makes our printer work again, changes that light bulb that burned out, or adds air to our car tires. While we can surely attend to these things ourselves, taking care of each other is one of the joys in life, and showing you care about her in these ways will make her happy.

Like most people, we women need time to ourselves. Know when to give your lady space. Smothering her with your love will read more like low self-esteem than romance. Trust her and don't get jealous. If your intentions are truly honorable, you need to be able to trust that hers are as well. Jealous men don't get to keep dating me, and most women feel the same way.

A gentleman reassures his lady about his feelings toward her, and communicates clearly. Trust me; this is going to prevent miscommunications and a whole lot of headaches for you. Communicate your feelings openly, honestly and clearly. We women can overthink things and come to conclusions about things you said, especially if it seemed confusing or open to interpretation.

Women will sit around analyzing what you meant by something, inevitably reading things into it what you could have meant. "What do you think he meant by that?" is a commonly heard question from fellow women. To avoid this pitfall, it's important that you tell the truth and reassure her. Do not leave your woman filling in the dots. Reassure, communicate and be honest. People find out the truth in the end, and no relationship can withstand dishonesty.

When you've been dating long enough to know how you feel about her, let her know how much she means to you and express that there's no one else you'd rather be with. If you don't mean it, you need to get honest with yourself about your intentions. Dragging things out with her is disrespectful and unfair to everyone involved.

Extend your chivalry to her friends and family. You're sure you really care about her and your intentions are honorable? Great. Then show respect and interest in the important people in her life. Make an effort to get to know them in the same ways you did with her, by listening, communicating and showing you care. She will notice and appreciate these efforts on your part. It's also important to women to be introduced to your friends. Let them know how special she is to you. An honorable man doesn't keep his woman a secret.

A real gentleman is a gentleman across the board. Show maturity. Crude humor and offensive language shouldn't leave the locker room. Send her an email using full words, without abbreviations like "lol." A lady wants to know that she's dating a man, not a teenager. Don't talk about other women you are interested in or how great your ex was to your new woman. And, rest assured your lady doesn't want to hear how hot the waitress was at dinner. Also, don't hit on women the moment you're apart from your lady (refer back to intentions), as it will not lead to a satisfying relationship with your sweetheart.

Gentlemanly behavior is especially important on social media platforms, too. What you do and say can be tracked, and can lead to big trouble in relationships. Liking every hot picture your gal pals and former lovers post to Facebook is probably not going to leave your lady trusting you. Openly flirting online is disrespectful to your sweetie. Don't do things online that will hurt her feelings or have her questioning yours.

If you really are crazy about your lady and know that you want to be with just her, and then show the maturity and courage to commit to her. This is an important step in showing honorable intentions and being a true gentleman. Good luck!

Antonia Hall, M.A., is a writer, artist, and communications professional from the Bay Area who's committed to helping people awaken to joyfully following their heart's calling and living their highest potential. She has lived in the Netherlands, France, Mexico, and Costa Rica, and loves to explore new lands and cultures. She completed her M.A. at the Institute of Transpersonal Psychology in Palo Alto. She is the owner of Antonia Hall Communications. She is completing her first book. For more information, see soulatwork.com *and* odewire.com.

How to Make an Uninterested Woman Become Interested (By A Woman)

Jessica Claire
New York Dating Coach

Make an uninterested woman become interested by finding out why the woman doesn't want to date you and working to improve yourself in different areas. Avoid trying to date a woman who is uninterested because of unchangeable circumstances with advice from a professional dating coach in this free video on dating advice for men.

Hi, this is Jessica Claire with New York Dating Coach in New York City. In this clip, we're going to talk about how to make an uninterested woman become interested.

Now, first, figure out why she's not interested. If it's something obvious like, "Well, you don't make enough money" or "You don't have the same political view as I do," then maybe it can't be helped. Maybe there's nothing you can do to change that. However, if her disinterest is based on something very obvious, for example, "Well, you know, you don't necessarily dress yourself appropriately" or "You're always late" or "I could never date someone who…" et cetera, then work on that particular part of yourself.

If she's the kind of woman that you want to date, maybe all women of her stature aren't going to be interested. You can always, always improve yourself, and if you're constantly working to do so, it's most likely going to improve your dating life. Also, decide if someone who's that uninterested is someone that you really want. Are you ever going to truly win her over? If not, maybe it's time to move on. This is Jessica Claire in New York City.

www.ehow.com/video_4950840_make-uninterested-woman-become-interested.html.

Read more: www.ehow.com/video_4950840_make-uninterested-woman-become-interested.html#ixzz2YEHMADCI

How to Treat Your Wife

Carol Naumann

This poem is for husbands, filled with good advice on how to treat your wife.

One you should treasure, but not as a possession,
Who needs to be loved, not treated with aggression?
Her value is more than all the world's treasures,
Not just the sum of scale's unit measures.
She should always be built up, not torn down,
By all the words you speak, when she is around.
She needs to be hugged and not pushed away,
Especially when you're both having a bad day.
Words spoken to her in haste and anger,
Can place her fragile heart in danger.
She should be admired for her boundless love,
And looked upon as a true gift from Above.
Not used as a target for all your frustration,
But held close and kissed with loving admiration.
You should always appreciate her commitment to you,

And not take for granted what she's given up for you!
Kiss her and love her all that you possibly can,
And don't be embarrassed to be seen holding her hand.
Treasure each day as if it were the last,
So at the end of your life you're not regretting your past.

Copyright Carol Naumann.
Reprinted from www.FamilyFriendPoems.com with permission of the author.

www.ingramcontent.com/pod-product-compliance
Lightning Source LLC
LaVergne TN
LVHW051227070526
838200LV00057B/4633